JIM THOME

Lefty Launcher

by

Amy Rosewater

SPORTS PUBLISHING INC.
www.SportsPublishingInc.com

In memory of Dave Lidecka, one of the best sports editors around, and in thanks to Dennis Manoloff and my husband, Marc Halushka.

Series editor: Rob Rains
Cover design: Christina Cary
Photo editor: Terrence Miltner
Project manager: Jay Peterson
Cover photos: AP/Wide World Photos

ISBN: 1-58261-251-X
Library of Congress Catalog Card Number: 00-101299

SPORTS PUBLISHING INC.
www.SportsPublishingInc.com

Printed in the United States.

CONTENTS

Jim Thome's high socks became a trademark for the 1997 Indians. (Joe Robbins Photography)

CHAPTER ONE

Socks Up

When Jim Thome turned 27, his Cleveland Indians teammates gave him a celebration he would never forget.

That night, August 27, 1997, the Indians played the Anaheim Angels. One by one, the Indians walked onto the field to their respective positions just as they always did. Jim, meanwhile, remained on the bench. A left-handed hitter, Jim sometimes would sit against left-handed pitchers.

As Jim looked out to the field from the dugout, he noticed something wasn't quite right. Everyone was at their usual positions: Omar Vizquel at shortstop, Matt Williams at third base and Sandy Alomar Jr. was crouched behind the plate. But they all looked a little bit different.

Virtually all of his teammates were dressed like him, with their red socks hiked up to the knees. On most days, Jim is the only member of the Indians who wears his socks knee-high in games. Jim began wearing them that way in the minors, as a tribute to old-time baseball and to his dad and grandfather, who also wore their socks high.

Now the tables had turned; his teammates were saluting him. Maybe those socks would help them hit 40 home runs, as Jim ultimately did that season.

"They looked good," Jim said, smiling.

Jim approved of the way his teammates looked, but he liked the way they played even more. They hit like Jim that night, scoring 10 runs in the fourth inning against the Angels and winning, 10-4. Leading up to that game, the Indians had been in a funk. Indians manager Mike Hargrove was under fire and few in Cleveland were optimistic about the team's chances of returning to the World Series.

After that game, everything turned in Cleveland's favor. The victory pushed the Indians to a three-game lead in the American League Central Division standings. Cleveland closed with an 18-14 record and upset the New York Yankees and Baltimore Orioles to reach the World Series.

Who knew what an impact those socks would have?

"I was the ringleader," Indians outfielder David Justice told Paul Hoynes of *The* (Cleveland) *Plain Dealer*. "It was something for Thome's birthday. Something for the team, something to show a little unity."

Aside from his socks, Jim also contributed 40 home runs to the Indians' season in 1997. (AP/Wide World Photos)

A one-day spoof turned into a season-long battle cry. The next game, Hargrove and the coaching staff wore their socks high. When the Indians returned home for a three-game series against the Chicago Cubs, the grounds crew sported knee-high socks, too.

The fans also got into the act. Some wore buttons saying "Socks Up" and "Get Knee High in Cleveland." It seemed everyone wanted to be like Jim.

"I don't know why it took so long," said Kevin Seitzer, the Indians first baseman. "But as silly as it sounds, those socks brought people together."

The socks became the symbol of a new spirit in the Cleveland Indians clubhouse. Perhaps more than anyone, Jim noticed the change.

"To be honest," Jim said, "I don't think we can say that all season long we've been having fun

While Jim celebrated scoring this run in Game 6 of the World Series, the Marlins won the series four games to three. (AP/Wide World Photos)

around here. But recently, it's been different. We're having fun."

Jim never imagined he would be the team's fashion trend-setter. Nor did he expect his socks to be a reason why the team got out of its season-long funk and into the World Series.

It didn't matter to Jim that the team might have intended, at least initially, to poke a little fun at his socks. As long as the team was winning, Jim wouldn't care if they wore socks on their heads. In Jim's mind, winning was the bottom line. After all, the Indians paid him to hit home runs and lead the team to championships, not for his good looks.

Following in his family's footsteps, Jim (standing next to the coach on the left) showed early potential hitting five home runs and six doubles in 13 games in the West Peoria Little League.

CHAPTER TWO

From the Midwest to the Majors

Growing up in the heart of the Midwest in Peoria, Illinois, Jim was raised on sports. And baseball was at the base of his family tree. His father played fast-pitch softball. His grandfather played in the Three-I League, a minor league that had teams in Iowa, Indiana and Illinois. His aunt, Carolyn Thome Hart, is in the National Softball Hall of Fame.

Jim's fondest memories were the trips he made with his dad to see the Chicago Cubs play in Wrigley Field. Peoria is a couple of hours southwest of Chicago, so driving to see the Cubs was always a special treat for Jim. He would see the Cubs play and dream of being a major-leaguer.

The youngest in a family of five children (twin sister, Jenny, is two minutes older than Jim), Jim grew up watching brothers Chuck and Randy excel in basketball and baseball. Jim didn't want to be as good as them—he wanted to be better. At the dinner table Jim would ask his mom how much milk his brothers drank when they were his age. She'd tell him, and he'd respond by drinking even more. He wanted to be bigger and stronger.

Still, no one seemed to believe in Jim except himself.

"I remember when he was little he said he'd

make it to the major leagues," said Jim's mom, Joyce. "He said, 'I'm going to make it. I'm not going to work.'"

"He told us that forever," said Jim's dad, Chuck. "But it was all wishing and hoping."

Even though Jim was a standout player in high school, no major league teams drafted him. Undrafted but not undetermined, Jim continued to play baseball, hoping his dream would come true.

Jim decided to play at Illinois Central Junior College for a year so he could go through the draft again in 1989. No one paid much attention to him until he played in a junior college game in Chicago.

"There were a bunch of scouts there, but they'd all come to see another player," Indians scout Tom Couston told Paul Hoynes of the Plain Dealer. "Thome was playing at shortstop and he went 1-

An odd conversation with a scout led to Jim being drafted in the 13th round of the 1989 draft. (Joe Robbins Photography)

for-4, or maybe it was 0-for-4. But every ball he hit was a rocket. His swing was so quick and powerful that I was surprised he didn't kill somebody."

Couston wanted to make sure the other scouts didn't catch on to his secret find. So he quietly asked the coach to bring Jim over to talk.

"First of all, the coach sent over the wrong kid," Couston said. "I told him, 'I don't want you.' When Thome came over I didn't want any other scouts to see me talking to him. So we're standing back-to-back. Jimmy kept calling me sir and turning around to talk to me and I kept saying, 'Don't look at me. Keep looking off into the distance.' He probably thought I was wacko."

Couston's stealth worked, because the Indians drafted Jim in the 13th round of the 1989 draft. And Jim proved to be one terrific find.

Jim's (No. 25) continued hard work, after not making a minor-league roster, eventually got Jim into the minors. (Courtesy of the Charlotte Knights)

3

Hard-Working Man

After the Indians signed Jim, he did not get complacent or have an inflated opinion of himself. After all, he had not reached his ultimate goal of playing in the big leagues. Whatever it took to make the majors, Jim was going to do—and then some.

Right off the bat, the Indians created a strength and conditioning program to make Jim bigger. Jim called his dad about the regimen and said, "I'm going to double what they tell me to do."

His dad told him not to overdo it and just follow the team's program. But Jim, a hard-working

Charlie Manuel not only helped Jim get into the minor leagues, he also managed Jim in Colorado Springs and Charlotte. The two would be reunited when Charlie was named manager of the Indians for the 2000 season. (Courtesy of the Charlotte Knights)

man who longed to play before the hard-working, blue-collar fans of Cleveland, wouldn't listen.

"When he reported to spring training, the Indians, well . . . they were aghast," Chuck Thome said. "I was positive about him. I knew it was his dream."

Despite the extra effort, Jim didn't make any of the Indians minor-league rosters when spring training ended. That's when most players realize their dream is over. True to form, Jim didn't take no for an answer and stayed in Winter Haven, Florida, for extended spring training. As it turned out, it probably was the best thing that could have happened to him.

If the Indians had assigned Jim to the minors, he would not have met Charlie Manuel. A former Indians hitting instructor, Manuel spent time after spring training to work with hitters. At the time, he was focused on developing a young first baseman. No one paid much attention to Jim at first. But he

With some help from a popular baseball movie, Jim became a "natural" at hitting the ball into right field during his time with the Charlotte Knights. (Courtesy of the Charlotte Knights)

paid close attention to everyone else. He watched the two men work and followed Manuel's every move. Pretty soon, Manuel took notice.

"In those two weeks, Thome started hanging out rockets all over the place," Manuel said. "I said to myself, 'Maybe I better start paying attention to this guy.'"

Manuel is glad he did, and the two became almost as close as father and son. In 1991, Manuel was Jim's Triple-A manager in Colorado Springs. On September 4, Manuel turned him over to the majors for the first time. Jim debuted for the Indians in Minnesota as the starting third baseman, going 2-for-4 with an RBI and run scored. His first hit was a single off Tom Edens.

Jim played 27 games for the Indians that September, batting .255. He appeared in 40 games for Cleveland in an injury-riddled 1992, batting .205.

The next year, Manuel again was Jim's Triple-A manager, in Charlotte, North Carolina. That season, Manuel became frustrated by his prized pupil. He couldn't figure out how to teach Jim, a left-handed hitter, to hit a ball to right field. Even Manuel's coaches were stumped. Then Manuel saw the movie, "The Natural," which stars Robert Redford as a left-handed batter from yesteryear who could pull the ball with authority. When Redford came to the plate for an at-bat, he'd point the bat toward the field, then bring it back.

Manuel thought it might be worth having Jim use the same approach. If life could imitate art, Manuel would have one great ballplayer on his hands.

It did, and he did.

Using his Redford-style swing, Jim led the International League with a .332 average and 102 RBI and was third in the league with 25 home runs. He earned the Lou Boudreau Award as the Indians' top minor-league position player, and also played in 47 games for the Indians. Everything was coming into place naturally.

Even after Jim made the majors he maintained a strong relationship with Manuel. When Jim was in a hitting slump, Manuel, the Indians hitting instructor, was there to help him get through it.

Jim always wanted to return the favor. So when Manuel was named to replace Mike Hargrove as the Indians manager on November 2, 1999, Jim went out of his way to support Manuel in his new job just as Manuel did for Jim when he was starting out.

Jim had been on an outdoors vacation in Michigan with pitcher Steve Karsay when he found out Manuel got the job as manager. Jim and Steve cut their trip short to be at Manuel's side.

"He deserved this," Jim said. "My wife told me this must be an important day for me to come back early from a hunting trip. This is a good day for the Indians organization."

In addition to his skills on the field, his teammates and fans appreciate all the good things Jim also does off the field. (AP/Wide World Photos)

CHAPTER FOUR

A Good Guy

Some players change when they reach the big leagues. They are praised and lauded and earn a lot of money, which makes them think they are more important than everyone else. But even as Jim emerged as a star with the Indians, he never let fame go to his head. He always tried to be the same old Jim who grew up in Peoria.

Maybe it's because he knew how hard it was for him to reach the big leagues. Maybe it's because of an experience he had when he first met major-league players at age 8. It's probably a little bit of both.

One day Jim and his dad drove from their home in Peoria to see their favorite team, the Chicago Cubs. Jim hoped he would get an autograph from his hero, Dave Kingman. Before the game, Jim approached Kingman for an autograph. Kingman walked a few steps toward Jim but then turned away and never even said a word to him. Several other Cubs players signed autographs for Jim that day, but Kingman left a lasting impression on him.

Jim remembers the incident when young baseball fans approach him for autographs. They look at him the way he once looked at Kingman, and Jim doesn't want to let anyone down. In his mind, being a famous ballplayer means you follow through on those types of things.

"What makes us feel so good is that Jim comes out of the clubhouse and takes time to sign and talk with the kids," said Jim's dad. "That's just the way he is."

Jim doesn't just sign autographs for kids. For the past two Christmases, he has dressed up as Santa while his wife, Andrea, plays the role of Mrs. Claus. The Thomes collect toys in a Cleveland-area mall and Jim signs autographs to everyone who donates a toy. Then they deliver the presents to needy children around Cleveland.

In December 1999, Thome was scheduled to spend two hours at the mall signing for toys. However, when the second hour ended, there still were fans in line. Jim did not flinch. He could have gotten up and departed, and no one would have complained because he fulfilled his obligation. But Jim stayed and signed until everybody was satisfied. In fact, Jim took care of another dozen fans on his way to the car. He wound up signing for almost three hours.

"I couldn't believe what I was seeing," said one fan, who drove one hour to exchange three toys for three autographs. "You hear about athletes arriving late and leaving early at signings. And when they do sign, they don't look at you or talk to you. Not Thome. He smiled and talked to everybody, especially the kids. He never made you feel like he wanted to be somewhere else, and he stuck around until everyone was taken care of. That's special."

That's just Jim being Jim, who also has served as an honorary co-chairman of the United Way Home Run Derby for the last three seasons.

Jim's down-to-earth charm has made him sought-after in the Cleveland community. For the past four years, he has been a spokesman for the Royal Auto Family, a Cleveland-owned car dealership. Not only does Jim appear in TV ads for the company, but he helps write some of the commercials, too. The ads have been so popular that owner

Steve Derin attributes more than half of his sales growth to Jim.

"We like people like Jim Thome, who's great with kids," Derin told the *Plain Dealer.* "Credibility is a big part of this business and I think this gives us an edge."

Jim has become such a hero in Cleveland that he even has created his own website (http://www.TeamThome.com) to accommodate admirers. Amazingly, fans from as far away as Finland have logged onto the Internet to check out Jim's site. The website offers everything from T-shirts to Jim's trademark red socks; proceeds are donated to charity.

Cleveland has become home to Jim and Andrea, but he also has a residence back in Peoria. Even though he has made it as a professional athlete, he has never forgotten his roots. In the off-season, Jim continues to make charitable contributions to his hometown.

In Peoria or Cleveland, Jim is recognized. Fans at gas stations and golf courses stop to talk to him. He is very approachable, even though he doesn't have to be. It's just the way he is.

Jim never puts on a superstar air. It's the reason he is so well liked by the media, too—and it's not always an easy bunch to please. It is not uncommon to see Jim as the first player in the Indians locker room being interviewed after a game, or the last to leave.

Some players like to hide from reporters, especially after a bad game. They'll sneak off to the weight room, where reporters are off-limits, or simply leave without a word. Jim is different. Win or lose, he makes himself available to answer questions. And Jim never has been known to belittle or laugh at someone for what might seem like a stupid question.

"The players have a job to do, and so does the media," Jim says.

He understands his role as a professional baseball player and is one of the most genuine guys in the game. After the 1995 season, he won the Frank Gibbons-Steve Olin Good Guy Award, an honor given to the player or staff member who is most helpful to reporters covering the Cleveland Indians.

It's no wonder why Jim has been embraced by so many.

Jim originally broke into the majors as a third baseman. Here he tags out Marquis Grissom at third in the 1995 World Series. (AP/Wide World Photos)

Breaking In

Jim's first full season in the majors in 1994 didn't come without its share of trials and tribulations. He proved he was an offensive threat by hitting 20 homers and driving in 52 runs in 98 games. Defense, however, was another story.

He broke into the majors as a third baseman. Every time he would throw to first base, it was an adventure. Jim committed 15 errors that season. Fans called the local sports radio station almost on a daily basis to complain about Jim's poor fielding.

Newspaper articles suggested Jim should return to the minor leagues and learn to play first base.

Some players might have taken the fans' displeasure hard and their careers would have suffered. Jim turned their comments into a challenge. Still, the criticism was hard to ignore.

"At times, it was tough," Jim told Tony Grossi of the *Plain Dealer.* "When you're making mistakes and you're with a team that's winning and in a race, it's hard to pick yourself up."

When major-league baseball shut down that season because of a strike, some players went on vacation. Others tried to help negotiate a deal with the team owners. Jim spent it by working on his fielding. When the strike ended and the Indians were in spring training the following year, he fielded up to 200 balls a day from Tribe infield coach Buddy Bell.

"He needed support and people to believe in him," Bell said. "The problem he had early on was that he was worried about throwing the ball before he caught the ball. The thing that really helped him was that he cut down on his steps after he caught the ball before throwing it."

As Jim continued to solve the defensive problems, one image stuck out in his mind. He remembered how teammate Omar Vizquel made three errors on Opening Day 1994. One of the best defensive shortstops of all-time, Vizquel was stunned by the mishaps and so was everyone else in Jacobs Field.

"He never went anywhere to hide after that game," Jim recalled. "He went back to his locker and later won a Gold Glove. I watched how he faced everybody straight on and I thought, 'What a class guy.' I wanted to be like that. You don't see that too much anymore."

Despite any fielding errors he made, Jim's bat made him a valuable member of the Cleveland Indians. (Joe Robbins Photography)

Like Omar, Jim is not the type of player who played baseball simply to cash a paycheck. He wanted to get better, and he did. Jim committed 17 errors in 1995, and although he was far from being a Gold Glove third baseman, he showed definite improvement. The fans liked his attitude and rallied around him.

It didn't hurt that he hit .314 with 25 home runs and 73 RBI that season. Or that he helped lead the Indians to their first World Series in 41 years, either. But Jim always keeps his success in perspective. He knows how hard it was for him to gain respect in the majors, and he was never going to forget that.

There was a lot to celebrate for Jim and the Indians in 1995. (AP/Wide World Photos)

Reaching The Playoffs

When Jim signed with the Indians in 1989, Cleveland was one of the worst teams in baseball. They had not been to the World Series since 1954 and had not won the world championship since 1948.

Comedians used to make their living by telling jokes about how bad the Indians were, and there was a generation of Indians fans that didn't know what it was like to see a winner. In 1989, the Indians finished 73-89. Two years later, they lost 105 games.

But in Jim's eyes, he couldn't have signed with a better organization. With General Manager Hart as the architect, the Indians built a young, power-hitting team that would change baseball in Cleveland. Players such as Jim, Albert Belle, Carlos Baerga, Kenny Lofton and Sandy Alomar Jr. would capture the city's heart and rekindle its passion for the game.

The biggest change happened when the Indians moved from Municipal Stadium to Jacobs Field in 1994. From the first moment the players stepped inside Jacobs Field for Opening Day, the place seemed magical. The team went 66-47 and was in the hunt for a playoff spot. But the Indians' dreams of playing in the World Series disappeared because of the strike and the playoffs were canceled.

Jim and his teammates vowed to pick up in 1995 where they left off after the strike-shortened 1994 season. Featuring one of the most lethal offensive lineups in baseball, the Indians dominated the Central Division. They won 17 games in their last at-bat, keeping Clevelanders glued to the team's every pitch and swing. On numerous occasions, Jim's bat was at the beginning, middle or end of the comebacks.

The Indians finished with 100 victories that season. The Kansas City Royals finished second in the division, but were 30 games out of first place. The Indians' three stars—Albert Belle, Kenny Lofton and Carlos Baerga—all put up big numbers. Belle hit 50 home runs and 52 doubles; Lofton led the American League with 54 steals; and Baerga batted .314 with 90 RBI. Jim did his part, too. He established career-highs in home runs (25), hits (142) and RBI (73).

In their first trip to the postseason in 41 years, the Indians made quick work of the Boston Red Sox, sweeping the division series in three games.

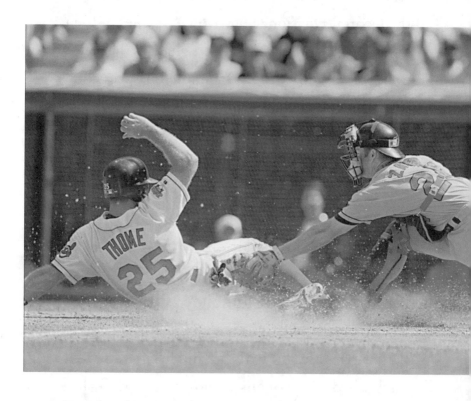

Jim played an important role in the Indians getting to the World Series in 1995, including hitting a game-winning home run in Game 5 of the ALCS. (AP/Wide World Photos)

Although the Indians played well, Jim hit .154 (2-for-13) and had just one RBI. When the Indians played against the Seattle Mariners in the American League Championship Series, however, he was one of the stars.

Jim hit the game-winning home run in pivotal Game 5, a two-run shot off Chris Bosio in the sixth that propelled the Indians to a 3-2 lead in the series. The ball landed in the middle deck of the right-field seats in Jacobs Field. Jim gave one of his bats to the fan who caught the ball, in exchange for the prized momento. He then gave the ball to his parents.

The series wasn't over yet, though, and the Indians had to travel back to Seattle to try to wrap things up. In Game 6, right-hander Dennis Martinez threw seven shutout innings and the Indians beat Seattle and ace Randy Johnson, 4-0. The

Indians were going to the World Series for the first time since 1954.

"This is great," Jim said while being doused with champagne by his teammates in the locker room following the big victory. "This is one of the best feelings I've ever had. It's just a big pleasure to be playing with these guys."

The Indians faced the Atlanta Braves in the World Series, a daunting matchup even for their prolific hitters. The Braves had perhaps the game's toughest rotation in Greg Maddux, Tom Glavine, John Smoltz and Steve Avery. That didn't seem to bother Jim in the least. "It's going to be awesome," he said. Jim simply was glad to be going to the World Series, period.

The Indians did not start out well against the Braves. They lost the first two games in Atlanta and barely beat the Braves, 7-6, in Game 3 in Jacobs Field. The Braves won Game 4 and held a commanding 3-1 lead in the best-of-seven World Series.

With Atlanta one more victory from a world championship, the Indians needed to beat ace pitcher Greg Maddux to keep their chances alive. After his teammates knocked out Maddux, Jim hit a majestic home run off Atlanta reliever Brad Clontz in the eighth inning. It sailed 436 feet into the center-field picnic area in Jacobs Field to give the Indians a 5-2 lead; they held on to win, 5-4, and force a Game 6.

Jim tossed the bat aside and as he rounded the bases, proudly lifting one arm in the air. "It's the World Series," Jim said afterward. "I got caught up in the emotion of the moment."

As it turned out, Jim and the Indians only postponed an Atlanta celebration. The Braves won Game 6, 1-0, behind Glavine and a home run by David Justice (who later was traded to Cleveland).

Cleveland fans embraced Jim and the Indians after the World Series and looked forward to the next year. (Joe Robbins Photography)

Even though the Indians had lost the World Series, Clevelanders embraced the team. Fans lined up at the airport to greet the players when they returned from Atlanta, and the city held a parade the next day. About 30,000 fans showed up downtown to cheer them on. "We love you, Indians!" they shouted.

As happy as they were, Jim and his teammates wanted to make the city even happier by winning it all the next season.

With the success of 1995, Jim was excited about the 1996 season. (AP/Wide World Photos)

CHAPTER SEVEN

Giving it Another Go

The 1995 season was like a dream, and Jim did not want to wake up. When he arrived in spring training in 1996, he eagerly anticipated a return to the World Series. His enthusiasm was dampened when the Indians traded pitcher Mark Clark to the New York Mets.

Jim and Mark were best friends. As teammates with the Indians, they always made sure to reserve hotel rooms next to each other. In the off-season, they spent a lot of time together, too. Jim's home in Peoria is only about 35 minutes away from Clark's in Bath, Illinois. Not only do the two enjoy base-ball, but both are avid outdoorsmen.

The trade took its toll on Jim. In the first nine games of the season, Jim scratched out one hit and he didn't have a home run until his 47th at-bat. Jim didn't say anything to reporters about how much he missed having his best friend around the club-house until later that season.

"Losing Mark Clark was like losing a brother to me," Jim admitted. "(The trade) was tougher probably for him than for me because at least I had an environment that I was used to. But I didn't have any friends on the team quite like him. I just never met a guy whom I had so much in common with. Even my own mother said I looked like Mark. It took a while, but I adjusted."

By the end of April, Jim's average improved to .299 and by the All-Star break, he was hitting .310 with 16 home runs and 51 RBI. He didn't make the American League All-Star team, which he had hoped, but Jim proved his offense didn't leave when Clark did.

In the second half of the season, Jim moved up in the batting order from sixth to third. The move helped him immensely, especially because pitchers didn't want to face the Indians' No. 4 batter, Albert Belle. "When I was batting sixth and seventh, I may have gotten one good fastball to hit," Jim said. "Now I get maybe three good fastballs."

During the 1996 season, Belle and the Indians were having trouble negotiating a contract extension. If Jim had any say in the matter, he would have done what he could to keep Belle in the lineup.

"I get a lot better pitches to hit with Albert Belle behind me," Jim said. "If I had the money, I'd give it to help sign Albert Belle because he's going to help me with my career, too."

Jim gets congratulations from teammate David Justice after scoring. (AP/Wide World Photos)

Jim did so well with Albert batting behind him that on August 25, Milwaukee Manager Phil Garner made the unusual move of having his pitcher intentionally walk Jim to load the bases and face Albert instead. Right-hander Doug Jones came to the mound to pitch to Albert, who singled in two runs. The move surprised everyone. No one could ever remember any team walking a player to get to Albert. Everyone was caught off-guard, including Jim.

"That showed a lot of respect for me," Jim said. "When I walked to first base, I thought, 'I have arrived.'"

*With all of the success, the fans are firmly behind Jim
and the Indians. (AP/Wide World Photos)*

Try, Try Again

The 1996 season didn't end the way the Indians hoped it would. Instead of returning to the World Series, they were defeated by the Baltimore Orioles in the division series. The Indians had a much longer off-season than they had planned. There would be no fanfare or parade this year.

Although they were disappointed, Cleveland baseball fans didn't give up on the team. They bought all of the tickets for the 1997 home games in a matter of nine days. Clevelanders had waited a long time to see good baseball. They weren't going to give up on a good thing that easily.

For Jim, 1997 was a season of starting over. The Indians acquired third baseman Matt Williams in a trade with San Francisco. Bringing Matt to town meant Jim would have to move to first base.

When Indians General Manager John Hart broached the subject of changing positions with Jim, there wasn't much of an argument. Jim didn't talk to his agent. He didn't call his parents, either. He discussed it with no one. He knew two things: He didn't want to make waves and he wanted to win. He also knew that he might never play in the All-Star Game because there are so many talented first basemen in the majors.

If John Hart asked Jim to pitch for the team, he probably would.

"If it helps the team win," he told Paul Hoynes of the *Plain Dealer,* "I'm there. I believe that what goes around, comes around. If you help people now, they're going to help you later."

Just as he had in the past when he struggled defensively, Jim put in extra hours to make the transformation from a third baseman into a first baseman. He went to Chain O' Lakes Park, the Indians' spring-training home in Winter Haven, Florida, two hours before most of his teammates arrived at 8 a.m. to work with coaches Johnny Goryl and Brian Graham. As usual, Jim set high goals for himself.

"I want to be the best," he said. "I may never be an All-Star . . . but that's irrelevant. The bottom line is winning a ring. If that means I've got to go across the diamond to let Matt Williams play, fine."

Jim also had the benefit of having a former first baseman as his manager—Mike Hargrove. A 12-year major leaguer, Hargrove helped Jim make the transition. "We don't want to overload him with

Jim, in the background, runs up to join pitcher Jose Mesa, front, and catcher Sandy Alomar in celebrating their playoff win over the Baltimore Orioles in 1997. (AP/Wide World Photos)

too much information," Hargrove said. "The thing that's great about Jimmy is that if he doesn't understand something, he'll just hand you his glove and say, 'Here, show me how to do it.'"

Jim proved to be a more than adequate first baseman and, as usual, hit the baseball hard. He hit a career-high 40 home runs and had 102 RBI. Perhaps one of the most impressive statistics he registered was 120 walks, making him the first Indian in history to draw 100 or more walks in consecutive seasons. Jim always has recognized that, while there are times to swing for the moon, patience is also a virtue in this game.

Although Jim didn't make the initial All-Star team cut, American League manager Joe Torre of the New York Yankees selected Jim to the team when David Justice suffered a hyperextended left elbow. Jim did not get a hit in his lone at-bat, but he got a chance to achieve his dream of being an All-Star.

Better yet, he got to be an All-Star in front of fans in Cleveland. The fans in Jacobs Field loved seeing Jim in the lineup. When he took batting practice for the Home Run Derby, he was showered with applause.

Once the regular season resumed, the Indians again won the Central Division. But this time Cleveland was not quite as dominant. Sure, the Indians had the talent to do well, but the team was criticized for being lethargic. It was hard to blame the Indians. After all, it was difficult to get motivated to play against sub-.500 teams like Minnesota and Kansas City. The Indians wanted to play against the best in baseball and win it all.

The Indians seemed to find the inspiration they needed in Jim's socks. After losing Game 1 against the hated Yankees in New York, the Indians went on to win three of the next four games to clinch the division series. Jim made a sensational diving stop of a Paul O'Neill grounder in deciding Game 5, turning it into a force play that helped preserve a 4-3 lead.

The Indians won a wild rematch against the Baltimore Orioles, four games to two, to clinch the American League pennant and a second trip to the World Series. Cleveland got to the World Series almost in spite of Jim. In the division series and American League Championship Series, Jim hit .138 (4-for-29). But he came to life when the team faced the Florida Marlins. In the World Series, he hit two home runs.

As good as the Indians were, they weren't good enough. The World Series went to a seventh game. In the ninth inning, the Indians held a 2-1 lead. The Indians were two outs away from winning their first World Series title since 1948, but the Marlins tied the game and wound up winning the title two innings later. It was a painful end. Jim

For the second time, Jim had been to the World Series and came up short in 1997. (AP/Wide World Photos)

sat on the dugout bench and buried his head is hands.

Once again, the city held a rally in the team's honor on Euclid Avenue—a main street in downtown Cleveland. A sign read, "1997 World Class Champions."

It was a nice gesture, but the players knew it would have been nicer if they had truly been champions. David Justice was one of the main speakers and he praised Jim in front of all the fans that listened. "He has the strength of about eight gorillas," Justice said.

Jim grinned, but inside he didn't feel so strong. Coming so close, yet being so far, was tough to take. Jim knew another season lay ahead and the team would try again, but he didn't know if he'd ever have a championship ring on his finger.

Even with Jim hitting four home runs, it wasn't enough to get the Indians past the Yankees in the 1998 ALCS. (AP/Wide World Photos)

9

Becoming A Star

By the time the 1998 season came, virtually everyone in Cleveland knew who Jim was. Fans wore his No. 25 jersey in Jacobs Field and they liked Jim for his hard-working ways.

In the national scheme of things, however, Jim had not reached superstardom. By the time the All-Star Game was held in Denver, Mark McGwire and Sammy Sosa were chasing Roger Maris' record of 61 home runs, and Ken Griffey Jr. was not far behind. Jim was having an exceptional season of his own, hitting .326 with 23 home runs and 73 RBI, but those numbers couldn't compare to those of McGwire, Sosa and Griffey.

Still, Jim was having a strong enough season that the fans voted him into the All-Star Game for the first time in his career. He was thrilled to be an All-Star and he was even more excited about being selected to participate in the Home Run Derby again. He couldn't wait to test his home-run swing in the thin Colorado air.

Griffey did not share that attitude. Even though he led the American League with 35 home runs at the All-Star break, he refused an invitation to the competition. Only after a crowd of 51,000 fans in Coors Field booed Griffey during batting practice, did the Seattle star change his mind.

Griffey, McGwire and Sosa were the obvious favorites. But as it turns out, Jim powered his way through the opening rounds of the competition and wound up facing Griffey in the finals. McGwire, surprisingly, was eliminated in the first round. Griffey beat Jim, three homers to two, but Jim was not the least upset by the loss.

On his way to being eliminated, Jim smashed a handful of bombs deep into the upper deck in Coors Field. It caused national TV announcers to gasp.

"That was great," Jim said. "That was fun."

It was also a bit of relief. When Jim was in the Home Run Derby before a hometown crowd in Jacobs Field in 1997, he failed to hit a single homer.

"If I didn't hit at least one homer," Jim said, "my teammates would have been on me forever."

Jim continued to belt home runs after the break and was on pace for 42 home runs and 118 RBI. But his stellar season came to a halt when Tampa Bay pitcher Wilson Alvarez hit him with a pitch

After competing in the home run contest, Jim continued to hit more home runs, including this home run in the ALCS against the Yankees. (AP/Wide World Photos)

August 7. Jim broke his right hand and missed the next six weeks.

It was a tough break for the team to take. "You don't take 29 homers and 82 RBI out of your lineup and not miss them," Hargrove said.

Jim saw the silver lining amidst the bad news. "It's just one of those things," he said. "At least I can come back for the playoffs."

But it drove Jim crazy not to be playing. He would rather be in an 0-for-20 slump than be out of the lineup. He went through rehabilitation in the minors and finally was healthy enough to play again, on September 16. In his first at-bat in 35 games, Jim made a 402-foot announcement that he was back. He hit a solo home run and was greeted with cheers and handshakes from his teammates when he returned to home plate.

Jim could not have scripted his return any better. The Indians beat Minnesota, 8-6, to clinch their fourth consecutive Central Division title. "I couldn't have picked a better night to come back," Jim told Liz Robbins of the *Plain Dealer* as teammates sprayed his back with champagne. "Words can't describe what I felt like coming to home plate. It was awesome."

Even his teammates, who have long known Jim's hitting prowess, were impressed. "I don't know how he does it," said Manny Ramirez. Jim's return was a powerful reminder to the Indians of how valuable he is to the team. Richie Sexson, a young prospect who filled in for Jim while he was sidelined, put it best: "Everybody knows that, in order for us to go to the World Series and do what we need to do, we need Jim Thome."

The Indians were thankful Jim was back in the lineup for the postseason. Although he hit just .237 in the playoffs, he had a team-high six homers and 10 RBI in 10 games—four of his home runs were against the New York Yankees in the American League Championship Series. Jim's power surge wasn't enough to get the Indians back to the World Series, though. The Yankees beat Cleveland, four games to two, and went on to sweep the San Diego Padres for the championship. The only losses New York had in its postseason run were against Cleveland. And the Yankees knew they were lucky to get past Jim and the Indians.

Jim continued his power hitting in 1999 including this grand slam he hit against the Oakland Athletics. (AP/ Wide World Photos)

Just Dial 511

There are home runs and there are monster home runs. Jim hits both kinds. The big homers are the ones that separate the stars from the ordinary players. Mark McGwire has made a career out of hitting rockets way out of ballparks.

Jim put himself among the top power hitters in the game on July 3, 1999. On that day, he hit a 511-foot home run off Kansas City's Don Wengert. He hit the ball so hard, it bounced off a pillar to the right of the center-field bleachers in Jacobs Field and caromed into the street through an iron fence.

Baseball fans that witnessed Jim's homer in Jacobs Field that day didn't need a calculator to know it was a titanic shot. Nor did his fellow Indians.

"I don't think I've ever seen a ball hit that far," Hargrove said.

That's because he hadn't. Before Jim hit that home run, the longest homer in Jacobs Field was a 485-foot drive by McGwire that bounced off a sign above the bleachers. Not only was Jim's home run longer than McGwire's, but it was longer than any other home run hit by a Cleveland Indian. Luke Easter hit a 477-foot home run in the old Cleveland Stadium on June 23, 1950.

"It was a fluid swing," Jim said. "It was nice. Maybe I should slow down and swing like that more often."

Jim was happy he could get his hands on the ball as a keepsake. A fan gave the ball to Indians officials in exchange for an autographed bat and ball and four tickets to another Indians game. Again, Jim encased the ball to give his family.

The next day, another fan held up a sign saying, "511" during Jim's first two at-bats. Jim didn't repeat that mammoth feat, but long will be remembered for it.

The thunderous homer was part of a regular season in which he batted .277 with 33 homers, 108 RBI and 101 runs scored in 146 games—terrific numbers, but not quite up to Jim's standards. What fans, and even teammates, did not realize was that Jim played in pain for most of the season. Observers did not necessarily know about his bad back because Jim did not want them to know. He did not want anyone to feel sorry for him, or to think he was making excuses.

Even suffering from a bad back, Jim still hit 33 home runs, drove in 108 runs, and scored 101 runs himself. (AP/Wide World Photos)

The back got better by the end of the season, and Jim vowed to be even more productive in 2000.

Jim plays even better in October. He hit this grand slam against the Red Sox in the 1999 AL division series. (AP/Wide World Photos)

in Good Company

There's something about October that gets Jim's juices flowing. It's the time of year when he can sense the World Series is attainable. The air gets crisp and the tension gets tight.

Hitting a home run against Detroit in May is one thing. Hitting one against the New York Yankees in October is another. Any baseball player worth his contract lives for a chance to hit a home run when it matters most. To Jim, playing in October is why he loves this game.

"Why wouldn't you look forward to this?" he said. "Why wouldn't you accept the challenge, with everybody watching, with the best competition? This is something you should see as fun, as something special in your life."

Reggie Jackson will long be remembered as "Mr. October" because he was so successful in the playoffs. He and another former New York Yankee, Mickey Mantle, are the game's all-time postseason home run leaders with 18. Jim is close to surpassing them both with 16 through 1999. Babe Ruth finished his career with 15.

Reggie Jackson, Mickey Mantle and Babe Ruth are legends. They're Hall of Famers. Jim is a player who might not have made it to the big leagues if a scout hadn't noticed him in a junior college game. Even he is stunned that he is associated with players of that stature. "I am a guy from Peoria, Illinois," Jim said. "Never, ever, growing up as a kid did I think my name would someday be mentioned in the same sentence with guys like Babe Ruth, Mickey Mantle or Reggie Jackson."

Some might say that Jim would not be in such elite company if baseball didn't add the division series in 1995. Jackson, Mantle and Ruth didn't have as many opportunities each season to hit home runs in the playoffs. Still, Jim hit his 16th home run in his 50th postseason game. Jackson needed 77 games and Mantle needed 65 games to hit 18. Ruth had 15 home runs in 41 games.

To top it off, Jim is the only player to ever hit two postseason grand slams. His first was off David Cone in Game 6 of the 1998 American League Championship Series against the New

***Even with all the impressive numbers Jim has put up in
the postseason, he will not be satisfied until he wins the
World Series. (AP/Wide World Photos)***

York Yankees. The second came against Boston's John Wasdin in the second game of the 1999 division series.

Ever since the Indians emerged as an American League powerhouse in 1995, Jim has been coming up big in October. In 1995, he hit four home runs—including the one off Brad Clontz in Game 5 of the World Series.

The only postseason in which Jim didn't hit a home run was 1996. That's when he suffered a broken right hand in the first game of the division series against Baltimore. Despite the pain, he played the remainder of the series and batted .300. The Orioles won the series, robbing Jim of any other opportunities to hit the long ball that season.

In 1997, he only batted .211 but had two postseason homers. He hit six home runs in 1998 and had four more in 1999. Jim hit his 15th and 16th postseason homers in the Indians' final game of the century. In the critical Game 5 of the division series against Boston, Jim homered to give Cleveland a 3-2 lead. Later, he hit a two-run shot off the hard-throwing Derek Lowe to deep center field for an 8-7 lead. Unfortunately for the Indians, Jim's home-run hitting wasn't enough. After jumping to a 2-0 lead in the series, the Red Sox won the final three games to eliminate the Indians from the postseason.

Jim could do nothing but hang his head after that final game, a 12-8 defeat. He gave it everything he had. The long balls just couldn't go long enough. Afterward, reporters asked him about his place in postseason history. How did it feel to be among baseball's great home-run hitters? As usual, Jim tried his best to answer the question.

"The individual numbers are great." he said, "But the postseason is not about numbers. It is about winning. I want to win a World Series."

With Jim's talent, the potential is always there.

Jim Thome Quick Facts

Full Name: James Howard Thome
Team: Cleveland Indians
Position: First Base
Jersey Number: 25
Bats: Left
Throws: Right
Height/Weight: 6-4/225
Hometown: Peoria, Illinois
Birthdate: August 27, 1970

Drafted: By Indians in the 13th round of the 1989 draft.

1999 Highlight: Jim broke his own club record by drawing 127 walks. He also led the American League in walks and strikeouts (171), the first player to do so since 1958.

Stats Spotlight: Jim hit three over 30 home runs for the fourth straight season in 1999. He is the only left-handed batter in Indians history to accomplish that.

Little-Known Fact: Jim was All-State in both basketball and baseball in high school.

Jim Thome's Career Hitting Statistics

Year	G	AB	R	H	2B	3B	HR	RBI	BB	AVG	OBP	SLG
1991	27	98	7	25	4	2	1	9	5	.255	.298	.367
1992	40	117	8	24	3	1	2	12	10	.205	.275	.299
1993	47	154	28	41	11	0	7	22	29	.266	.385	.474
1994	98	321	58	86	20	1	20	52	46	.268	.359	.523
1995	137	452	92	142	29	3	25	73	97	.314	.438	.558
1996	151	505	122	157	28	5	38	116	123	.311	.450	.612
1997	147	496	104	142	25	0	40	102	120	.286	.423	.579
1998	123	440	89	129	34	2	30	85	89	.293	.413	.584
1999	146	494	101	137	27	2	33	108	127	.277	.426	.540
Totals	916	3077	609	883	181	16	196	579	646	.287	.412	.547

Year	SO	TBB	IBB	HBP	SH	SF	GDP	SB	CS	SB%
1991	16	5	1	1	0	0	4	1	1	.500
1992	34	10	2	2	0	2	3	2	0	1.000
1993	36	29	1	4	0	5	3	2	1	.667
1994	84	46	5	0	1	1	11	3	3	.500
1995	113	97	3	5	0	3	8	4	3	.571
1996	141	123	8	6	0	2	13	2	2	.500
1997	146	120	9	3	0	8	9	1	1	.500
1998	141	89	8	4	0	4	7	1	0	1.000
1999	171	127	13	4	0	4	6	0	0	.000
Totals	882	646	50	29	1	29	64	16	11	.593

Jim Thome's Career Fielding Statistics

First Base

Year	G	PO	A	E	DP	FPct	LeagueFPct
1997	145	1233	95	10	123	.993	.992
1998	117	998	85	10	97	.991	.992
1999	111	931	81	6	93	.994	.992
Totals	**373**	**3162**	**261**	**26**	**313**	**.992**	**.992**

Third Base

Year	G	PO	A	E	DP	FPct	LeagueFPct
1991	27	12	60	8	6	.900	.955
1992	40	21	61	11	3	.882	.950
1993	47	29	86	6	10	.950	.951
1994	94	62	173	15	12	.940	.948
1995	134	75	214	16	22	.948	.952
1996	150	86	262	17	24	.953	.956
Totals	**492**	**285**	**856**	**73**	**77**	**.940**	**.952**

1999 American League Strikeouts Leaders

Jim Thome	171
Dean Palmer	153
Troy Glaus	143
Carlos Delgado	141
Jose Canseco	135

1999 American League Walks Leaders

	BB	IBB
Jim Thome	127	13
Jason Giambi	105	6
John Jaha	101	2
Albert Belle	101	15
Bernie Williams	100	17

1999 American League Home Run Leaders

Ken Griffey, Jr.	48
Raphael Palmiero	47
Manny Ramirez	44
Carlos Delgado	44
Shawn Green	42
Alex Rodriguez	42
Juan Gonzalez	39
Dean Palmer	38
Matt Stairs	38
Albert Belle	37
Ivan Rodriguez	35
John Jaha	35
Jose Canseco	34
Jim Thome	**33**
Mo Vaughn	33
Jason Giambi	33

Baseball Superstar Series Titles

Collect Them All!

Football Superstar Series Titles

Collect Them All!

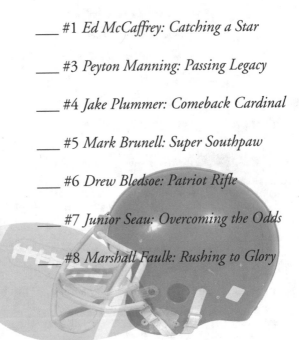

___ #1 *Ed McCaffrey: Catching a Star*

___ #3 *Peyton Manning: Passing Legacy*

___ #4 *Jake Plummer: Comeback Cardinal*

___ #5 *Mark Brunell: Super Southpaw*

___ #6 *Drew Bledsoe: Patriot Rifle*

___ #7 *Junior Seau: Overcoming the Odds*

___ #8 *Marshall Faulk: Rushing to Glory*

Only $4.95 per book!

Basketball Superstar Series Titles

Collect Them All!

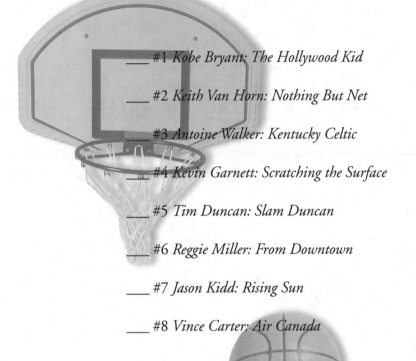

____ #1 *Kobe Bryant: The Hollywood Kid*

____ #2 *Keith Van Horn: Nothing But Net*

____ #3 *Antoine Walker: Kentucky Celtic*

____ #4 *Kevin Garnett: Scratching the Surface*

____ #5 *Tim Duncan: Slam Duncan*

____ #6 *Reggie Miller: From Downtown*

____ #7 *Jason Kidd: Rising Sun*

____ #8 *Vince Carter: Air Canada*

Only $4.95 per book!

Racing Superstar Series Titles

___ #1 *Jeff Gordon: Rewriting the Record Books*

___ #2 *Dale Jarrett: Son of Thunder*

___ #3 *Dale Earnhardt: The Intimidator*

___ #4 *Tony Stewart: Hottest Thing on Wheels*

Hockey Superstar Series Titles

___ #1 *John LeClair: Flying High*

___ #2 *Mike Richter: Gotham Goalie*

___ #3 *Paul Kariya: Maine Man*

___ #4 *Dominik Hasek: The Dominator*

___ #5 *Jaromir Jagr: Czechmate*

___ #6 *Martin Brodeur: Picture Perfect*

Only $4.95 per book!

Collect Them All!